CW01305317

Young Billionaire's Cryptocurrency Journey

Insights and Strategies for Success

MICHAEL PAGE

MICHAEL PAGE

Copyright © 2024 Michael Page

All rights reserved.

ISBN: 979-8-3230-0640-3

First Edition: April, 2024

No part of this publication may be reproduced, distributed, or transmitted in any form or by any means, including photocopying, recording, or other electronic or mechanical methods, without the prior written permission of the publisher, except in the case of brief quotations embodied in critical reviews and certain other noncommercial uses permitted by copyright law.

MICHAEL PAGE

Table of Contents

Introduction 5

From Teenage Crypto Trader to Mega Billionaire: My Journey in the Digital Frontier 9

Chapter 1: Introduction to Cryptocurrencies for those in their 20s and 30s: 15

    Case Study: The Rise of Bitcoin 19

Chapter 2: Understanding Blockchain Technology 22

    Case Study: Ethereum and Smart Contracts 27

Chapter 3: Getting Started with Cryptocurrencies................... 30

    Case Study: Jane's Journey into Cryptocurrency................... 57

Chapter 4: Popular Cryptocurrencies 60

Chapter 5: Investing in Cryptocurrencies 68

    Case Study: David's Investment Strategy............................... 73

Chapter 6: Using Cryptocurrencies in Everyday Life 77

    Case Study: Anna's Experience with Crypto Payments 81

Chapter 7: Legal and Regulatory Considerations 86

    Case Study: Crypto Regulation in Different Jurisdictions 92

Chapter 8: Advanced Topics 97

    Case Study: Decentralized Autonomous Organizations (DAOs) 102

Chapter 9: Risks and Security Measures 107

    Case Study: The Mt. Gox Hack 112

Chapter 10: The Future of Cryptocurrencies 118

    Case Study: Central Bank Digital Currencies (CBDCs).......... 123

MICHAEL PAGE

Interview Questions with Responses from Michael Page 128

Practical Tips and Strategies for Beginners.............................133

Conclusion...139

Glossary 144

About the Author 158

MICHAEL PAGE

Introduction

Welcome to the world of cryptocurrencies, where digital innovation meets financial revolution. In recent years, cryptocurrencies have captured the attention of millions around the globe, sparking curiosity, excitement, and sometimes confusion. Whether you're a seasoned investor or someone who's just heard about Bitcoin for the first time, this book is your essential guide to navigating the fascinating realm of digital currencies.

In this introduction, we'll explore what cryptocurrencies are, why they matter, and what you can expect to learn from this book.

Cryptocurrencies are a form of digital or virtual currency that uses cryptography for security and operates on a decentralized network known as blockchain. Unlike traditional currencies issued by governments and central banks, cryptocurrencies are not controlled by any single entity. Instead, they rely on a distributed ledger technology that records all transactions transparently and securely.

The rise of cryptocurrencies represents a paradigm shift in how we perceive and interact with money. By eliminating the need for intermediaries like banks and payment processors, cryptocurrencies offer a more efficient, transparent, and inclusive financial system. They empower individuals to take control of their wealth, facilitate borderless transactions, and unlock new opportunities for innovation and economic empowerment.

However, with great promise comes great responsibility. The world of cryptocurrencies is complex and rapidly evolving, filled with opportunities as well as risks. Scams, volatility, regulatory uncertainties—these are just some of the challenges that crypto enthusiasts must navigate.

But fear not! This book is designed to be your roadmap through this exciting and sometimes daunting landscape. Whether you're curious about the technology behind cryptocurrencies, interested in investing, or simply looking to understand how they might impact the future of finance, you've come to the right place.

In the chapters that follow, we'll delve into the fundamentals of cryptocurrencies, explore popular digital assets like Bitcoin and Ethereum, discuss how to buy, store, and use cryptocurrencies safely, and examine the potential risks and rewards of investing in this space. We'll also touch on advanced topics like mining, decentralized finance (DeFi), and non-fungible tokens (NFTs), giving you a comprehensive overview of the crypto ecosystem.

By the end of this book, you'll have the knowledge and confidence to navigate the world of cryptocurrencies with ease. Whether you're looking to make your first crypto purchase or simply expand your understanding of this transformative technology, I hope you find this book to be a valuable resource on your journey into the exciting world of digital money. Let's dive in!

MICHAEL PAGE

From Teenage Crypto Trader to Mega Billionaire: My Journey in the Digital Frontier

I never imagined that my journey into the world of cryptocurrencies would lead me to become a billionaire by the age of 20. It all started when I was just a curious 14-year-old with a passion for technology and a hunger for knowledge. Little did I know, my decision to dive into the world of digital currencies would change my life forever.

It all began with a simple Google search – "What is Bitcoin?" As I delved deeper into the rabbit hole of blockchain technology and decentralized finance, I was captivated by the endless possibilities and revolutionary potential of cryptocurrencies. With each passing day, I immersed myself in forums, articles, and online communities, absorbing as much information as I could about this emerging asset class.

At first, I started small – investing my pocket money into Bitcoin and other altcoins, learning the ropes of trading and investing through trial and error. Despite the volatility and uncertainty of the crypto market, I remained steadfast in my belief in the transformative power of digital currencies and blockchain technology.

As the years went by, my investments began to pay off. With each bull run and market cycle, my portfolio grew exponentially, and I found myself becoming more deeply entrenched in the world of cryptocurrencies. I experimented with different trading strategies, participated in initial coin offerings (ICOs), and even dabbled in mining and staking to maximize my returns.

But it wasn't just about the money – it was about the journey. Along the way, I forged connections with like-minded individuals from around the world, shared ideas and insights, and collaborated on projects that pushed the boundaries of what's possible in the crypto space. From decentralized applications and smart contracts to non-fungible tokens (NFTs) and decentralized finance (DeFi), I witnessed firsthand the incredible innovation and creativity that flourished in the digital frontier.

Looking back, I realize that starting early in crypto gave me a significant advantage. While others were hesitant to embrace this new and unfamiliar technology, I saw it as an opportunity to be at the forefront of a revolution – to be part of something bigger than myself. By starting young, I had the time, flexibility, and resilience to weather the ups and downs of the crypto market, to learn from my mistakes, and to seize the opportunities that presented themselves along the way.

But it wasn't all smooth sailing. I faced my fair share of challenges and setbacks – from market crashes and regulatory uncertainty to security breaches and hacking attempts. Yet, through it all, I remained determined and focused on my goals, knowing that the potential rewards far outweighed the risks.

Now, as a 20-year-old crypto billionaire, I find myself humbled by the magnitude of my success and grateful for the opportunities that crypto has afforded me. Yet, I also recognize the responsibility that comes with wealth – to give back to the community, to support projects and initiatives that promote financial inclusion and social impact, and to inspire others to dream big and pursue their passions fearlessly.

My journey in the world of cryptocurrencies is far from over. As I look to the future, I see endless possibilities and untapped potential waiting to be unlocked. Whether it's building the next generation of decentralized applications, investing in innovative projects, or advocating for the mainstream adoption of cryptocurrencies, I remain committed to pushing the boundaries of what's possible and leaving a lasting legacy in the digital frontier.

So to all the young dreamers and aspiring entrepreneurs out there, I say this: embrace the unknown, embrace the risks, and embrace the opportunities that await you in the world of cryptocurrencies. Start early, stay curious, and never stop believing in the power of technology to change the world – because you never know where your journey might take you.

Yours Truly

Michael Page

Chapter 1: Introduction to Cryptocurrencies for those in their 20s and 30s:

Welcome to the exhilarating world of cryptocurrencies! If you're in your 20s and 30s, chances are you've grown up in the digital age, where technology shapes almost every aspect of our lives. From the way we communicate and socialize to how we shop and entertain ourselves, the digital revolution has touched nearly every corner of the globe.

And at the heart of this revolution lies cryptocurrencies – digital assets that have captured the imagination of millions around the world, including many in your generation. But what exactly are cryptocurrencies, and why should they matter to you as a 20-year-old navigating the complexities of the modern world?

Cryptocurrencies are, in essence, digital or virtual currencies that use cryptography for security and operate on a decentralized network called blockchain. Unlike traditional forms of money issued and regulated by governments and central banks, cryptocurrencies are decentralized and operate independently of any single authority.

At its core, cryptocurrency embodies the spirit of decentralization and democratization. It's about taking control of your financial destiny, free from the constraints of traditional banking systems and government oversight. For a generation that values individual autonomy and self-expression, cryptocurrencies offer a powerful tool for financial empowerment.

But cryptocurrencies are more than just digital money – they represent a paradigm shift in how we think about value, trust, and ownership. With cryptocurrencies, you can send money across the globe in a matter of seconds, without the need for intermediaries like banks or payment processors. You can invest in digital assets that hold the potential for exponential growth, without the barriers to entry typically associated with traditional financial markets.

For a young adult just starting out in the world, cryptocurrencies offer a unique opportunity to participate in a global financial ecosystem that's inclusive, accessible, and driven by innovation. Whether you're interested in investing, entrepreneurship, or simply curious about the technology behind cryptocurrencies, there's something for everyone in this exciting space.

Of course, with great opportunity comes great responsibility. The world of cryptocurrencies can be daunting, with its own set of risks and challenges. From the threat of hacking and scams to the volatility of the market, there are pitfalls to navigate and lessons to be learned.

But fear not! With the right knowledge and guidance, you can navigate the world of cryptocurrencies with confidence and clarity. That's where this book comes in. Whether you're a seasoned crypto enthusiast or someone who's just dipping their toes into the water, this book is your essential guide to understanding and navigating the exciting world of digital money.

In the chapters that follow, we'll explore everything you need to know about cryptocurrencies, from the basics of blockchain technology to practical tips for buying, storing, and using digital assets safely. We'll dive into popular cryptocurrencies like Bitcoin and Ethereum, explore the potential of decentralized finance (DeFi), and discuss the impact of emerging trends like non-fungible tokens (NFTs).

By the time you finish this book, you'll have the knowledge and confidence to navigate the world of cryptocurrencies like a pro. Whether you're looking to invest in the next big thing, build decentralized applications, or simply stay informed about the latest developments in the crypto space, this book will be your trusted companion on your journey into the exciting world of digital money. So buckle up, and let's explore the future of finance together!

Case Study: The Rise of Bitcoin

In 2009, an anonymous individual or group using the pseudonym Satoshi

Nakamoto introduced Bitcoin, the world's first decentralized cryptocurrency. Bitcoin was created as an alternative to traditional fiat currencies, offering a peer-to-peer electronic cash system that operates on a decentralized blockchain network.

Bitcoin's journey began with its humble origins, as early adopters mined coins using basic computer hardware and software. Over time, Bitcoin gained traction and popularity among technologists, libertarians, and enthusiasts who saw its potential to disrupt the existing financial system.

As Bitcoin gained mainstream attention, its value skyrocketed, reaching highs that few could have predicted. The cryptocurrency's decentralized nature, limited supply, and censorship resistance appealed to investors seeking a hedge against inflation and economic uncertainty.

Bitcoin's rise to prominence also brought challenges, including scalability issues, regulatory scrutiny, and concerns about energy consumption. Despite these challenges, Bitcoin has endured and remained the dominant cryptocurrency in terms of market capitalization and adoption.

Today, Bitcoin is widely recognized as a digital store of value and a hedge against traditional financial assets. Its decentralized nature and transparent blockchain have inspired the creation of thousands of other cryptocurrencies, fueling innovation and experimentation in the digital finance space.

MICHAEL PAGE

Chapter 2: Understanding Blockchain Technology

Welcome to the fascinating world of blockchain technology – the backbone of cryptocurrencies and a revolutionary force in the digital landscape. In this chapter, we'll break down the fundamentals of blockchain in a way that's easy to understand, even for a 20-year-old just getting started on their journey into the world of cryptocurrencies.

So, what exactly is blockchain, and how does it work?

At its core, blockchain is a distributed ledger technology that enables the secure and transparent recording of transactions across a network of computers. Think of it as a digital ledger or database that stores a record of every transaction ever made in a secure, tamper-proof manner.

The key innovation of blockchain is its decentralized nature. Unlike traditional databases that are owned and controlled by a single entity, blockchain operates on a peer-to-peer network where every participant, or node, has a copy of the entire ledger. This decentralization ensures that no single entity has control over the network, making it resistant to censorship and manipulation.

But what makes blockchain truly revolutionary is its use of cryptographic techniques to secure and validate transactions. Each block in the blockchain contains a set of transactions, along with a unique cryptographic hash that links it to the previous block. This creates a chain of blocks, hence the name "blockchain," where every block is connected to the one before it, forming an immutable record of transactions.

The process of adding new blocks to the blockchain is known as "mining" or "validation." Miners use powerful computers to solve complex mathematical puzzles, which requires a significant amount of computational power. Once a puzzle is solved, the new block is added to the blockchain, and the transactions it contains are considered confirmed and irreversible.

One of the key benefits of blockchain technology is its transparency and security. Because every transaction is recorded on a public ledger that's visible to anyone on the network, it's virtually impossible to alter or tamper with the data without the consensus of the majority of participants. This makes blockchain ideal for applications where trust and transparency are paramount, such as financial transactions, supply chain management, and voting systems.

Another important feature of blockchain is its immutability. Once a transaction is recorded on the blockchain, it cannot be changed or deleted. This ensures that the integrity of the data is preserved over time, making blockchain a reliable and tamper-proof record-keeping system.

But blockchain is not without its limitations. One of the biggest challenges facing blockchain technology is scalability – the ability to handle a large number of transactions quickly and efficiently. As more transactions are added to the blockchain, the network can become congested, leading to delays and higher fees. However, ongoing research and development efforts are underway to address these scalability issues and improve the efficiency of blockchain networks.

In summary, blockchain technology is a groundbreaking innovation that has the potential to transform industries and revolutionize the way we think about trust, transparency, and security in the digital age. As a 20-year-old exploring the world of cryptocurrencies, understanding the fundamentals of blockchain is essential for navigating this exciting and rapidly evolving landscape. So whether you're interested in investing in cryptocurrencies, building decentralized applications, or simply curious about the technology behind the digital revolution, blockchain is a concept worth exploring further.

Case Study: Ethereum and Smart Contracts

Ethereum, launched in 2015 by Vitalik Buterin and a team of developers, introduced a groundbreaking innovation to the cryptocurrency world: smart contracts. Ethereum's blockchain is designed to execute programmable contracts automatically, without the need for intermediaries.

Smart contracts are self-executing agreements with predefined rules and conditions written into code. They enable decentralized applications (DApps) to automate complex processes, such as financial transactions, voting systems, and supply chain management, in a transparent and trustless manner.

One of the most famous use cases of Ethereum's smart contracts is the rise of decentralized finance (DeFi) applications. DeFi platforms leverage smart contracts to offer traditional financial services, such as lending, borrowing, and trading, without relying on centralized intermediaries like banks or exchanges.

The success of Ethereum and its smart contract functionality has paved the way for a new era of blockchain innovation. Developers and entrepreneurs are now exploring ways to leverage smart contracts for a wide range of applications, including gaming, healthcare, real estate, and identity management.

MICHAEL PAGE

Chapter 3: Getting Started with Cryptocurrencies

Congratulations! You've taken the first step into the exciting world of cryptocurrencies. In this chapter, we'll guide you through the process of getting started with cryptocurrencies, from setting up your first wallet to making your first purchase. By the end of this chapter, you'll be well on your way to becoming a savvy crypto user.

Setting Up a Wallet:

The first thing you'll need to do to get started with cryptocurrencies is to set up a digital wallet. Think of your wallet as your personal bank account for storing and managing your digital assets. There are several types of wallets available, each with its own unique features and security considerations.

Online Wallets: Online wallets, also known as web wallets, are hosted on the cloud and can be accessed from any device with an internet connection. They're convenient and easy to use, but they're also more susceptible to hacking and security breaches. Popular online wallets include Coinbase, Blockchain.com, and Binance.

How to Set Up Online Wallets

Setting up an **online wallet** for cryptocurrencies is a straightforward process that typically involves the following steps:

Choose a Wallet Provider:

Research and choose a reputable online wallet provider that supports the cryptocurrencies you plan to store. Popular online wallet providers include

Coinbase, Binance, Blockchain.com, and Trust Wallet.

Visit the Wallet Provider's Website:
Once you've chosen a wallet provider, visit their website to create an account. Look for a "Sign Up" or "Create Account" button and click on it to begin the registration process.

Complete the Registration Form:
Fill out the registration form with your personal information, such as your name, email address, and password. Some wallet providers may require additional verification steps, such as providing a phone number or verifying your identity with a government-issued ID.

Verify Your Email Address:
After completing the registration form, you'll typically receive a verification email from the wallet provider. Click on the verification link in the email

to verify your email address and activate your account.

Set Up Two-Factor Authentication (2FA):

To enhance the security of your online wallet, consider setting up two-factor authentication (2FA). Most wallet providers offer 2FA options, such as SMS codes, authenticator apps (like Google Authenticator), or hardware keys.

Access Your Wallet:

Once your account is set up and verified, log in to your online wallet using your email address and password. Some wallet providers may also require you to enter a verification code from your 2FA method.

Generate Your Wallet Addresses:

After logging in, you'll typically be prompted to generate wallet addresses for the cryptocurrencies you want to store.

Follow the instructions provided by the wallet provider to generate wallet addresses for each cryptocurrency.

Fund Your Wallet:

To start using your online wallet, you'll need to fund it with cryptocurrencies. Depending on the wallet provider, you may be able to deposit funds directly into your wallet from another exchange or wallet, or you may need to purchase cryptocurrencies through the wallet provider's platform.

Secure Your Wallet:

Take steps to secure your online wallet, such as enabling additional security features like multi-signature authentication or setting up recovery phrases.

Be cautious of phishing scams and never share your login credentials or private keys with anyone.

Monitor Your Wallet:

Regularly monitor your online wallet for any unauthorized transactions or suspicious activity.

Keep track of your balances and consider setting up notifications or alerts for important events, such as deposits or withdrawals.

By following these steps, you can set up an online wallet for cryptocurrencies and start securely storing and managing your digital assets. Remember to choose a reputable wallet provider, enable additional security features like 2FA, and practice good security hygiene to protect your funds from unauthorized access.

Mobile Wallets: Mobile wallets are apps that you can download and install on your smartphone. They offer a good balance of convenience and security, allowing you to access your funds on the go. Some popular mobile wallets include Trust Wallet, Atomic Wallet, and MyEtherWallet.

How to Set Up Mobile Wallets

Setting up a mobile wallet for cryptocurrencies is similar to setting up an online wallet and typically involves the following steps:

Choose a Mobile Wallet App:

Research and choose a reputable mobile wallet app that supports the cryptocurrencies you plan to store. Popular mobile wallet apps include Trust Wallet, Coinbase Wallet, Atomic Wallet, and MyEtherWallet (MEW).

Download the App:

Visit the App Store (for iOS devices) or Google Play Store (for Android devices) on your mobile device.

Search for the mobile wallet app you've chosen and download it to your device.

Install and Open the App:

Once the app is downloaded, open it on your mobile device to begin the setup process.

Create a New Wallet:

Look for an option to create a new wallet within the app and select it. Follow the instructions provided by the app to create a new wallet, which typically involves generating a new seed phrase or private key.

Secure Your Wallet:

After creating your new wallet, you'll be prompted to secure it with a strong password or PIN.

Some mobile wallet apps also offer additional security features, such as fingerprint or facial recognition authentication.

Backup Your Seed Phrase:

During the setup process, you'll likely be given a seed phrase (also known as a recovery phrase or mnemonic phrase). Write down your seed phrase and store it in a safe place offline. This seed phrase is crucial for recovering your wallet if you lose access to your device.

Fund Your Wallet:

To start using your mobile wallet, you'll need to fund it with cryptocurrencies. Depending on the wallet app, you may be able to deposit funds directly into your wallet from another exchange or wallet, or you may need to purchase cryptocurrencies through the app's built-in exchange feature.

Explore Additional Features:

Once your wallet is set up and funded, take some time to explore the additional features offered by the mobile app. Many mobile wallet apps offer features like built-in exchange services, portfolio tracking, and support for decentralized applications (DApps).

Secure Your Device:

Ensure that your mobile device is secure by keeping your operating system and apps up to date with the latest security patches and updates.

Be cautious of installing unknown apps or clicking on suspicious links to avoid malware and phishing attacks.

Monitor Your Wallet:

Regularly monitor your mobile wallet for any unauthorized transactions or suspicious activity.

Keep track of your balances and consider setting up notifications or alerts for important events, such as deposits or withdrawals.

By following these steps, you can set up a mobile wallet for cryptocurrencies and start securely storing and managing your digital assets on your mobile device. Remember to choose a reputable wallet app, backup your seed phrase, and practice good security hygiene to protect your funds from unauthorized access.

Hardware Wallets: Hardware wallets are physical devices that store your cryptocurrencies offline, away from the reach of hackers. They're considered one of the most secure options for storing large amounts of crypto. Popular hardware wallets include Ledger Nano S, Trezor, and KeepKey.

How to Set Up Hardware Wallets

Setting up a hardware wallet for cryptocurrencies is a secure way to store your digital assets offline. Here are the steps to set up a hardware wallet:

Purchase a Hardware Wallet:

Research and choose a reputable hardware wallet device from a trusted manufacturer. Popular options include Ledger Nano S, Ledger Nano X, Trezor One, and Trezor Model T. Purchase the hardware wallet device from the official manufacturer's website or authorized resellers to ensure authenticity and security.

Unbox and Prepare the Hardware Wallet:

Unbox the hardware wallet device and ensure that all components, including the device, USB cable, and instruction manual, are included.

Inspect the device for any signs of tampering or damage before proceeding with the setup process.

Connect the Hardware Wallet to Your Computer:

Use the provided USB cable to connect the hardware wallet device to your computer or mobile device.

Ensure that the device is securely connected and powered on before proceeding to the next step.

Initialize the Hardware Wallet:

Follow the on-screen instructions displayed on the hardware wallet device to initialize the device and set up a new wallet.

You may be prompted to choose a PIN code to secure the device and protect your funds from unauthorized access.

Write Down Your Recovery Seed Phrase:

During the setup process, you'll be given a recovery seed phrase (also known as a recovery seed, mnemonic phrase, or backup phrase).

Write down the recovery seed phrase provided by the hardware wallet device on the provided recovery sheet or a piece of paper. Ensure that you write it down accurately and keep it in a safe and secure location offline.

Confirm the Recovery Seed Phrase:

After writing down the recovery seed phrase, you'll typically be asked to confirm it by entering the words in the correct order on the hardware wallet device.

Double-check the recovery seed phrase to ensure accuracy before confirming it on the device.

Complete the Setup Process:

Once the recovery seed phrase is confirmed, the setup process for the hardware wallet is complete.

Follow any additional on-screen instructions provided by the hardware wallet device to finalize the setup and begin using the wallet to store and manage your cryptocurrencies.

Install the Wallet Software:

Depending on the hardware wallet device you've chosen, you may need to install wallet software on your computer or mobile device to interact with the device.

Visit the official website of the hardware wallet manufacturer to download and install the appropriate wallet software for your device.

Transfer Funds to the Hardware Wallet:

After setting up the hardware wallet, you can transfer funds from your exchange account or other wallets to the hardware wallet address provided by the device.

Follow the instructions provided by the wallet software to send funds to the hardware wallet securely.

Secure and Backup Your Hardware Wallet:

Once your funds are stored in the hardware wallet, securely store the device and recovery seed phrase in separate physical locations.

Regularly backup your hardware wallet by securely storing multiple copies of the recovery seed phrase in different secure locations.

By following these steps, you can set up a hardware wallet for cryptocurrencies and securely store your digital assets offline, providing an extra layer of protection against online threats and unauthorized access. Remember to choose a reputable hardware wallet device, securely store your recovery seed phrase, and practice good security hygiene to protect your funds from loss or theft.

Paper Wallets: Paper wallets are a form of cold storage where you print out your private keys and public addresses on a piece of paper. While they're secure from online hacks, they can be vulnerable to physical damage or loss. Use paper wallets with caution and make sure to store them in a safe place.

Steps on How to Set Up Paper Wallets

Setting up a paper wallet is a secure and offline method to store your cryptocurrencies. Here are the steps to set up a paper wallet:

Choose a Paper Wallet Generator:

Use a reputable paper wallet generator to create your paper wallet. Popular options include Bitaddress.org and WalletGenerator.net.

Ensure that you are using a trusted and secure website to generate your paper wallet to avoid potential scams or security risks.

Access the Paper Wallet Generator:

Visit the website of the paper wallet generator you've chosen using a secure and trusted internet connection. Be cautious of phishing scams and ensure that you are visiting the correct website by verifying the URL and checking for secure connections (HTTPS).

Generate a New Wallet:

On the paper wallet generator website, look for an option to generate a new wallet or create a new paper wallet. Follow the instructions provided by the website to generate a new paper wallet for the cryptocurrency of your choice.

Print the Paper Wallet:

Once the paper wallet is generated, you'll typically be provided with a printable version of the paper wallet containing the public address and private key.

Print the paper wallet on a secure and trusted printer using high-quality paper to ensure durability and longevity.

Securely Store the Paper Wallet: After printing the paper wallet, securely store it in a safe and secure location offline.

Consider using a fireproof and waterproof safe or a safety deposit box to store your paper wallet securely.

Protect the Private Key:

The private key is the most sensitive and important component of the paper wallet, as it provides access to your funds.

Take extra precautions to protect the private key from unauthorized access or theft. Avoid sharing it with anyone and consider encrypting it or storing it in a secure location separate from the paper wallet.

Transfer Funds to the Paper Wallet:

To add funds to the paper wallet, transfer the desired amount of cryptocurrency from your exchange account or other wallets to the public address provided on the paper wallet. Follow the instructions provided by your exchange or wallet to send funds to the public address securely.

Monitor Your Paper Wallet:

Regularly monitor the balance of your paper wallet using a blockchain explorer or wallet software to ensure that funds are received and transactions are processed correctly.

Be cautious of accessing your paper wallet from public or shared computers to avoid potential security risks.

Backup Your Paper Wallet:

Consider creating backups of your paper wallet by printing multiple copies or writing down the public address and private key on separate pieces of paper. Store backups of your paper wallet in secure and trusted locations offline to ensure redundancy and protection against loss or damage.

Use Caution When Redeeming Funds:

When you're ready to redeem or spend funds from your paper wallet, use caution and follow best practices for securely importing the private key into a digital wallet or exchange.

Be mindful of potential security risks and only redeem funds from your paper wallet using trusted and secure devices and connections.

By following these steps, you can set up a paper wallet for cryptocurrencies and securely store your digital assets offline, providing an extra layer of protection against online threats and unauthorized access. Remember to choose a reputable paper wallet generator, securely store your paper wallet, and practice good security hygiene to protect your funds from loss or theft.

Once you've chosen a wallet that suits your needs, follow the instructions to set it up and secure it with a strong password or PIN. Be sure to back up your wallet's recovery phrase or seed phrase, as this will allow you to restore access to your funds if you ever lose or forget your password.

Buying Your First Cryptocurrency:

Now that you have a wallet set up, it's time to buy your first cryptocurrency. There are several ways to purchase cryptocurrencies, including:

Cryptocurrency Exchanges:

Cryptocurrency exchanges are online platforms where you can buy, sell, and trade cryptocurrencies. Some popular exchanges include Coinbase, Binance, Kraken, and Bitfinex. To buy crypto on an exchange, you'll need to create an account, verify your identity, and deposit funds using a bank transfer or credit/debit card.

Peer-to-Peer Platforms: Peer-to-peer platforms like LocalBitcoins and Paxful allow you to buy cryptocurrencies directly from other users, bypassing the need for a centralized exchange. These platforms offer more privacy and flexibility but may also carry higher fees and greater risk of fraud.

Bitcoin ATMs: Bitcoin ATMs are physical kiosks that allow you to buy and sell cryptocurrencies using cash.

They're convenient and easy to use, but they typically charge higher fees compared to online exchanges.

Over-the-Counter (OTC) Desks: OTC desks are services offered by cryptocurrency brokers and exchanges for large volume trades. They cater to institutional investors and high-net-worth individuals looking to buy or sell large amounts of crypto in a single transaction.

Regardless of which method you choose, make sure to do your research and choose a reputable seller or exchange with a good track record of security and customer service.

Security Best Practices:

As a new crypto user, it's important to prioritize security to protect your funds from theft or loss. Here are some security best practices to keep in mind:

Enable Two-Factor Authentication (2FA) on your wallet and exchange accounts to add an extra layer of security to your login process.

Use strong, unique passwords for your wallet and exchange accounts, and consider using a password manager to generate and store your passwords securely.

Keep your wallet's recovery phrase or seed phrase in a safe and secure location, such as a fireproof safe or a safety deposit box.

Be cautious of phishing scams and never share your private keys, recovery phrase, or personal information with anyone online.

N.B.

Consider using a hardware wallet for storing large amounts of crypto, and only keep small amounts of crypto on online or mobile wallets for everyday use.

By following these security best practices, you can minimize the risk of

unauthorized access to your funds and
enjoy peace of mind knowing that your
crypto assets are safe and secure.

Case Study: Jane's Journey into Cryptocurrency

Jane, a recent college graduate, was
intrigued by the concept of
cryptocurrencies and decided to dip her
toes into the world of digital finance.
She started by researching different
cryptocurrencies and learning about
blockchain technology through online
courses and tutorials.

After gaining a basic understanding of
how cryptocurrencies work, Jane opened
an account on a reputable
cryptocurrency exchange and purchased
her first Bitcoin. She also set up a
secure hardware wallet to store her
digital assets safely offline.

As Jane continued to educate herself about cryptocurrencies, she diversified her investment portfolio by exploring other altcoins with promising technology and use cases. She also participated in decentralized finance (DeFi) platforms to earn passive income through yield farming and liquidity mining.

Over time, Jane's confidence and knowledge in cryptocurrencies grew, and she became an advocate for blockchain technology within her social circle. She shared her experiences and insights with friends and family, encouraging them to explore the world of digital finance and invest responsibly.

Conclusion:
Congratulations! You've successfully set up your first cryptocurrency wallet,

made your first purchase, and learned about the importance of security in the world of cryptocurrencies. In the next chapter, we'll dive deeper into the world of popular cryptocurrencies like Bitcoin and Ethereum, exploring their history, features, and potential for the future. So keep exploring, stay curious, and remember to always prioritize security as you navigate the exciting world of cryptocurrencies. Happy hodling!

Chapter 4: Popular Cryptocurrencies

Welcome to the world of popular cryptocurrencies – where digital innovation meets financial revolution. In this chapter, we'll explore some of the most well-known and widely-used cryptocurrencies, including **Bitcoin**, **Ethereum**, **Ripple**, **Litecoin**, and more. Whether you're a seasoned crypto enthusiast or someone who's just getting started, understanding these popular digital assets is essential for navigating the ever-changing landscape of the crypto market.

Bitcoin (BTC):

Bitcoin is often referred to as the original cryptocurrency, and for good reason. Created in 2009 by an anonymous individual or group of individuals using the pseudonym Satoshi

Nakamoto, Bitcoin introduced the world to the concept of decentralized digital currency. It operates on a peer-to-peer network powered by blockchain technology, allowing users to send and receive payments without the need for intermediaries like banks or payment processors. Bitcoin's limited supply of 21 million coins and its deflationary monetary policy have made it a popular choice for investors seeking a store of value and a hedge against inflation.

Ethereum (ETH):

Ethereum is more than just a cryptocurrency – it's a decentralized platform that enables developers to build and deploy smart contracts and decentralized applications (DApps). Created by Vitalik Buterin in 2015, Ethereum introduced the concept of programmable money, allowing developers to create custom tokens and execute complex transactions automatically. Ethereum's native cryptocurrency, Ether (ETH), is used to pay for transaction fees and computational services on the network. With its vibrant ecosystem of DApps and the potential for innovation in areas like decentralized finance (DeFi) and non-fungible tokens (NFTs), Ethereum has become one of the most popular and widely-used cryptocurrencies in the world.

Ripple (XRP):

Ripple is a digital payment protocol and cryptocurrency created by Ripple Labs in 2012. Unlike Bitcoin and Ethereum, which operate on decentralized networks, Ripple is designed for use by financial institutions and payment providers to facilitate fast and low-cost cross-border transactions. Ripple's native cryptocurrency, XRP, is used to facilitate transactions on the Ripple network and has gained traction as a solution for real-time gross settlement

(RTGS) and remittance services. While Ripple has faced regulatory challenges and criticism for its centralized nature, its technology has the potential to disrupt the traditional banking system and improve the efficiency of global payments.

Litecoin (LTC):

Litecoin is often referred to as the "silver to Bitcoin's gold" and was created in 2011 by Charlie Lee, a former Google engineer. Like Bitcoin, Litecoin is a peer-to-peer cryptocurrency that operates on a decentralized network powered by blockchain technology. However, Litecoin distinguishes itself from Bitcoin with faster transaction times and lower fees, making it ideal for everyday transactions and micropayments. Litecoin's supply cap of 84 million coins and its use of the Scrypt hashing algorithm also set it apart from Bitcoin. With its focus on scalability and usability, Litecoin has become one of the most popular cryptocurrencies for both investors and merchants alike.

Cardano (ADA):

Cardano is a third-generation blockchain platform that aims to address the scalability, interoperability, and sustainability issues faced by earlier blockchain networks like Bitcoin and Ethereum. Founded by Charles Hoskinson, one of the co-founders of Ethereum, Cardano takes a research-driven approach to blockchain development, with a focus on peer-reviewed academic research and formal verification methods. Its native cryptocurrency, ADA, is used for staking and participating in the network's consensus mechanism, known as Ouroboros. With its commitment to scientific rigor and its vision for a decentralized future, Cardano has gained a strong following among developers and enthusiasts alike.

Case Study: The Rise of Binance Coin (BNB)

Binance Coin (BNB), launched in 2017 by the cryptocurrency exchange Binance, quickly rose to prominence as one of the most popular cryptocurrencies in the market. Initially created as a utility token for discounted trading fees on the Binance exchange, BNB has since evolved into a multi-faceted digital asset with diverse use cases.

One of the key drivers of BNB's success is its integration into the Binance ecosystem, which includes a wide range of services such as spot and derivatives trading, decentralized exchange (DEX), token launches, and staking. BNB holders can use the token to access various features and services within the Binance platform, enhancing its utility and demand.

Another factor contributing to BNB's popularity is its strong community support and active development team. Binance regularly introduces new initiatives, such as Binance Launchpad for token sales and Binance Smart Chain for decentralized applications (DApps), to expand the utility and adoption of BNB.

As a result of its growing ecosystem and utility, BNB has experienced significant price appreciation over the years, making it one of the top-performing cryptocurrencies in terms of return on investment (ROI). BNB's success demonstrates the potential of exchange-based cryptocurrencies to create value and innovation within the broader cryptocurrency ecosystem.

Conclusion:

These are just a few of the many cryptocurrencies that exist in the ever-expanding crypto market. Whether you're interested in investing, building decentralized applications, or simply staying informed about the latest developments in the world of cryptocurrencies, understanding these popular digital assets is essential for navigating the exciting and rapidly evolving landscape of digital finance. So keep exploring, stay curious, and remember that the world of cryptocurrencies is constantly evolving – who knows what the next big thing will be!

Chapter 5: Investing in Cryptocurrencies

Welcome to the world of cryptocurrency investing – where opportunity meets risk, and potential rewards abound. In this chapter, we'll explore the basics of investing in cryptocurrencies, from understanding the risks and rewards to developing a strategy that works for you. Whether you're a seasoned investor or someone who's just getting started, understanding how to invest in cryptocurrencies is essential for navigating the dynamic and often volatile crypto market.

Understanding the Risks and Rewards:

Investing in cryptocurrencies can be highly rewarding, but it also comes with its fair share of risks. Here are some key factors to consider before diving into the world of crypto investing:

Volatility: Cryptocurrencies are known for their extreme price volatility, with prices sometimes fluctuating by double-digit percentages in a single day. While this volatility can lead to rapid gains, it can also result in significant losses if not managed properly.

Market Sentiment: Cryptocurrency prices are heavily influenced by market sentiment and investor psychology. Positive news or developments can lead to sharp price increases, while negative news or regulatory uncertainty can trigger sell-offs.

Regulatory Risks: The regulatory landscape for cryptocurrencies is still evolving, and changes in regulations or government crackdowns can have a significant impact on the market. It's important to stay informed about regulatory developments and how they may affect your investments.

Security Risks: Cryptocurrency exchanges and wallets are often targeted by hackers and cybercriminals. It's essential to take precautions to protect your investments, such as using secure wallets, enabling two-factor authentication, and avoiding suspicious websites and phishing scams.

Despite these risks, investing in cryptocurrencies also offers the potential for significant rewards. With the right strategy and mindset, you can capitalize on the opportunities presented by this emerging asset class.

Developing an Investment Strategy:

Before investing in cryptocurrencies, it's essential to develop a clear investment strategy tailored to your financial goals, risk tolerance, and time horizon. Here are some key considerations to keep in mind:

Do Your Research: Take the time to research different cryptocurrencies and their underlying technology, team, and use cases. Look for projects with strong fundamentals, a clear roadmap, and a dedicated community of supporters.

Diversification: Diversifying your crypto portfolio can help spread risk and reduce exposure to any single asset.

Consider allocating your investment across different cryptocurrencies, industries, and investment strategies to minimize the impact of volatility.

Dollar-Cost Averaging (DCA): Dollar-cost averaging is a strategy where you invest a fixed amount of money at regular intervals, regardless of price fluctuations. This approach can help smooth out the impact of market volatility and reduce the risk of buying at the wrong time.

Risk Management: Set clear investment goals and establish risk management measures, such as *stop-loss orders* and *position sizing*. Only invest what you can afford to lose, and avoid investing more than you're willing to lose in a single trade or asset.

Long-Term Perspective:

Cryptocurrency markets can be highly unpredictable in the short term, but they have shown significant long-term growth potential. Take a long-term perspective with your investments and focus on projects with strong fundamentals and real-world utility.

Case Study: David's Investment Strategy

David, a seasoned investor, decided to allocate a portion of his investment portfolio to cryptocurrencies as a hedge against traditional financial assets. He adopted a long-term investment strategy focused on fundamental analysis and diversification to manage risk and maximize returns.

David conducted thorough research on various cryptocurrencies, evaluating factors such as technology, team, community, market demand, and use cases. He prioritized cryptocurrencies with strong fundamentals and real-world utility, such as Bitcoin, Ethereum, and other top-performing projects with promising technology and adoption.

To minimize risk and maximize diversification, David allocated his investment across multiple cryptocurrencies, balancing high-risk/high-reward assets with more stable and established ones. He also practiced disciplined risk management by setting clear investment goals, diversifying across different asset classes, and rebalancing his portfolio regularly.

Despite market volatility and short-term fluctuations, David remained focused on his long-term investment thesis and avoided succumbing to emotional impulses or FOMO (fear of missing out). He maintained a patient and disciplined approach, knowing that cryptocurrencies are a nascent asset class with the potential for significant growth over time.

As the cryptocurrency market evolved, David adjusted his investment strategy accordingly, staying informed about market trends, regulatory developments, and emerging opportunities. By staying disciplined, diversified, and informed, David successfully navigated the cryptocurrency market and achieved his investment goals.

Conclusion:

Investing in cryptocurrencies can be both thrilling and challenging, with the potential for significant rewards as well as risks. By understanding the basics of cryptocurrency investing, developing a clear investment strategy, and staying informed about market trends and developments, you can navigate the dynamic world of crypto investing with confidence and resilience. Remember to always do your own research, manage your risks responsibly, and stay focused on your long-term financial goals. With patience, discipline, and a willingness to learn, you can harness the power of cryptocurrencies to build wealth and achieve financial freedom in the digital age. Happy investing!

Chapter 6: Using Cryptocurrencies in Everyday Life

Welcome to the exciting realm of using cryptocurrencies in your everyday life – where digital money meets real-world applications. In this chapter, we'll explore the various ways you can use cryptocurrencies for payments, investments, and other practical purposes. Whether you're a seasoned crypto enthusiast or someone who's just getting started, understanding how to use cryptocurrencies in your daily life can open up a world of possibilities and opportunities.

Payment Methods and Services: One of the most common ways to use cryptocurrencies in everyday life is for making payments and transactions. Many merchants and businesses around the world now accept cryptocurrencies as a form of payment, allowing you to buy goods and services with digital assets. From online retailers and travel agencies to restaurants and coffee shops, the number of businesses accepting cryptocurrencies is steadily growing, providing you with more options for using your digital money in the real world.

In addition to traditional merchants, there are also specialized payment services and platforms that cater specifically to cryptocurrency users. These platforms offer features like cryptocurrency debit cards, which allow you to spend your crypto assets at any merchant that accepts traditional debit or credit cards. Some popular cryptocurrency payment services include BitPay, Coinbase Card, and Crypto.com.

Cryptocurrency ATMs and Debit Cards:

Cryptocurrency ATMs, also known as Bitcoin ATMs or BTMs, are physical kiosks that allow you to buy and sell cryptocurrencies using cash or traditional debit/credit cards. These ATMs provide a convenient way to convert between fiat currency and cryptocurrencies on the go, allowing you to access your digital assets anytime, anywhere. Cryptocurrency ATMs can be found in various locations, including airports, shopping malls, and convenience stores, making it easier than ever to buy and sell cryptocurrencies in your everyday life.

Similarly, cryptocurrency debit cards allow you to spend your crypto assets just like you would spend traditional money. These debit cards are linked to your cryptocurrency wallet and can be used to make purchases at any merchant that accepts debit or credit cards. Some cryptocurrency debit cards even offer additional features like cashback rewards and travel perks, making them a convenient and versatile payment option for crypto users.

Adoption and Future Outlook:

As cryptocurrencies continue to gain mainstream acceptance and adoption, the possibilities for using digital money in everyday life are only expected to grow. From online shopping and travel bookings to peer-to-peer payments and remittances, cryptocurrencies offer a fast, secure, and borderless alternative to traditional payment methods.

In addition to payments, cryptocurrencies also have the potential to revolutionize other areas of everyday life, such as identity verification, supply chain management, and voting systems. With the rise of blockchain technology and decentralized applications (DApps), we're likely to see even more innovative use cases for cryptocurrencies emerge in the years to come, further cementing their role as a transformative force in the digital age.

Case Study: Anna's Experience with Crypto Payments

Anna, a tech-savvy entrepreneur, decided to integrate cryptocurrency payments into her online e-commerce store to offer customers an alternative payment method. She implemented a payment gateway that supported popular cryptocurrencies like Bitcoin, Ethereum, and Litecoin, allowing customers to pay for products and services using their preferred digital assets.

By accepting cryptocurrencies as payment, Anna attracted a new customer base of crypto enthusiasts and early adopters who valued the convenience, security, and privacy offered by digital currencies.

Cryptocurrency payments also allowed Anna to tap into global markets and reach customers outside of traditional banking systems, expanding her business's reach and potential revenue streams.

To streamline cryptocurrency payments and mitigate price volatility, Anna implemented a payment processor that automatically converted cryptocurrencies into fiat currency at the time of purchase. This allowed her to receive stable fiat currency settlements while still offering customers the flexibility to pay with their preferred digital assets.

As word spread about Anna's acceptance of cryptocurrencies, her online store gained recognition within the cryptocurrency community and attracted media attention. Customers appreciated the seamless payment experience and the opportunity to support a forward-thinking business that embraced emerging technologies.

To further promote cryptocurrency adoption, Anna offered special discounts and promotions for customers who chose to pay with cryptocurrencies. These incentives encouraged more customers to explore cryptocurrency payments and experience the benefits firsthand, driving adoption and loyalty among her customer base.

As cryptocurrency payments became more mainstream, Anna expanded her payment options to include a wider range of digital assets and integrated additional features, such as recurring payments and subscription services. This allowed her to cater to the evolving needs and preferences of her customers while staying ahead of the curve in the rapidly evolving cryptocurrency landscape.

Overall, Anna's experience with cryptocurrency payments demonstrated the potential for businesses to leverage digital currencies as a means of payment and drive innovation in e-commerce. By embracing cryptocurrencies, Anna was able to differentiate her business, attract new customers, and stay competitive in a rapidly changing digital economy.

Conclusion:

Using cryptocurrencies in your everyday life can open up a world of possibilities and opportunities, allowing you to take control of your finances and embrace the future of money. Whether you're buying a cup of coffee, booking a flight, or sending money to a friend halfway across the world, cryptocurrencies offer a fast, secure, and convenient way to transact in the digital age.

As adoption and acceptance of cryptocurrencies continue to grow, we can expect to see even more innovative use cases and applications for digital money in the years to come. So whether you're a seasoned crypto enthusiast or someone who's just dipping their toes into the world of digital finance, now is the perfect time to explore the exciting possibilities of using cryptocurrencies in your everyday life. Happy spending!

Chapter 7: Legal and Regulatory Considerations

Welcome to the complex and ever-evolving world of legal and regulatory considerations in the realm of cryptocurrencies. In this chapter, we'll explore the various laws, regulations, and compliance measures that affect the use and adoption of cryptocurrencies, as well as the implications for individuals and businesses operating in this space. Whether you're a seasoned crypto enthusiast or someone who's just getting started, understanding the legal and regulatory landscape is essential for navigating the dynamic and sometimes murky waters of the crypto market.

Government Regulations Worldwide:

Cryptocurrencies operate in a regulatory gray area in many countries around the world, with governments grappling to define their legal status and establish clear regulatory frameworks. While some countries have embraced cryptocurrencies and blockchain technology with open arms, others have taken a more cautious or restrictive approach.

In the United States, for example, cryptocurrencies are subject to a patchwork of regulations at both the federal and state levels. The U.S. Securities and Exchange Commission (SEC) regulates cryptocurrencies and initial coin offerings (ICOs) as securities, while the Commodity Futures Trading Commission (CFTC) oversees cryptocurrency derivatives trading. Additionally, individual states may have their own regulations governing cryptocurrencies and blockchain technology.

Similarly, in Europe, the regulatory landscape for cryptocurrencies varies from country to country. Some European countries, like Switzerland and Malta, have adopted crypto-friendly regulations to attract blockchain startups and investment, while others have taken a more cautious approach, citing concerns about consumer protection and financial stability.

In Asia, countries like Japan and South Korea have implemented regulations to license and regulate cryptocurrency exchanges, while China has banned cryptocurrency trading and ICOs altogether. The regulatory landscape in Asia is constantly evolving, with countries taking different approaches to address the challenges and opportunities presented by cryptocurrencies.

Tax Implications:

In addition to regulatory considerations, cryptocurrencies also have tax implications that individuals and businesses need to be aware of. In many countries, cryptocurrencies are treated as property for tax purposes, meaning that they're subject to capital gains tax when bought, sold, or traded.

For individuals, this means keeping accurate records of cryptocurrency transactions, including the date of acquisition, the purchase price, and the sale price. Failure to report cryptocurrency transactions accurately can result in penalties or fines from tax authorities.

For businesses that accept cryptocurrencies as payment, there are additional tax considerations to take into account. In some jurisdictions, businesses may be required to convert cryptocurrency payments into fiat currency for tax reporting purposes, which can add an extra layer of complexity to accounting and compliance processes.

Staying Compliant:

Given the complex and evolving nature of cryptocurrency regulations, staying compliant with legal and regulatory requirements is essential for individuals and businesses operating in this space.

Here are some tips for staying compliant:

Stay Informed: Keep abreast of the latest regulatory developments and guidance from government agencies and regulatory bodies. Join industry associations and forums to stay connected with other professionals and experts in the field.

Consult Legal and Tax Professionals: Seek advice from legal and tax professionals who specialize in cryptocurrency law and taxation. They can help you navigate the legal and regulatory landscape and ensure that you're compliant with all applicable laws and regulations.

Implement Compliance Measures: Develop robust compliance policies and procedures to mitigate the risk of regulatory violations. This may include Know Your Customer (KYC) and Anti-Money Laundering (AML) procedures, as well as internal controls for monitoring and reporting suspicious activity.

Engage with Regulators: Build positive relationships with regulators and government agencies by proactively engaging with them and seeking guidance on compliance issues. Participate in industry consultations and working groups to contribute to the development of fair and effective regulations.

Case Study: Crypto Regulation in Different Jurisdictions

The regulatory landscape surrounding cryptocurrencies varies significantly from one jurisdiction to another, presenting challenges and opportunities for businesses and investors operating in the global cryptocurrency market. Let's explore the regulatory approaches of two different countries: the United States and Switzerland.

In the United States, cryptocurrencies are subject to a complex and evolving regulatory framework that encompasses federal and state laws, regulations, and enforcement actions. Regulatory agencies such as the Securities and Exchange Commission (SEC), Commodity Futures Trading Commission (CFTC), and Financial Crimes Enforcement Network (FinCEN) play key roles in overseeing different aspects of the cryptocurrency ecosystem.

The regulatory approach in the United States is characterized by a mix of enforcement actions, regulatory guidance, and legislative initiatives aimed at addressing consumer protection, investor safety, and financial stability concerns. However, the lack of clarity and consistency in regulations has created uncertainty for businesses and investors, hindering innovation and adoption in some cases.

In contrast, Switzerland has emerged as a crypto-friendly jurisdiction with a clear and favorable regulatory environment for cryptocurrencies and blockchain technology. The Swiss government and regulatory authorities have adopted a pragmatic and principles-based approach to regulation, focusing on promoting innovation while maintaining financial integrity and investor protection.

Switzerland's regulatory framework provides legal certainty and clarity for businesses and investors operating in the cryptocurrency space, encouraging innovation, investment, and entrepreneurship. The country's Crypto Valley in Zug has become a hub for blockchain startups and cryptocurrency projects, attracting talent and investment from around the world.

By comparing the regulatory approaches of different jurisdictions, businesses and investors can gain insights into the opportunities and challenges associated with operating in the global cryptocurrency market. Understanding the regulatory landscape is crucial for navigating compliance requirements, managing risk, and seizing opportunities for growth and expansion.

Conclusion:

Navigating the legal and regulatory landscape in the world of cryptocurrencies can be challenging, but it's essential for ensuring the long-term viability and legitimacy of the industry. By staying informed, consulting with legal and tax professionals, and implementing robust compliance measures, individuals and businesses can navigate the complexities of cryptocurrency regulations with confidence and integrity. As the regulatory landscape continues to evolve, it's crucial to remain vigilant and proactive in addressing emerging compliance challenges and opportunities.

Chapter 8: Advanced Topics

Welcome to the realm of advanced topics in the world of cryptocurrencies – where cutting-edge innovations and emerging trends shape the future of digital finance. In this chapter, we'll explore some of the most exciting and impactful developments in the crypto space, from mining and staking to decentralized finance (DeFi) and non-fungible tokens (NFTs). Whether you're a seasoned crypto enthusiast or someone who's just starting to explore the possibilities of digital money, understanding these advanced topics is essential for staying ahead of the curve and unlocking new opportunities in the world of cryptocurrencies.

Mining and Staking:

Mining and staking are two fundamental processes that underpin many blockchain networks, including Bitcoin and Ethereum.

Mining: Mining is the process of validating and adding new transactions to the blockchain by solving complex mathematical puzzles. Miners use powerful computers to compete for the chance to add a new block to the blockchain and receive a reward in the form of newly minted coins. Mining plays a crucial role in securing the network and maintaining the integrity of the blockchain.

Staking: Staking is an alternative consensus mechanism used by some blockchain networks, such as Ethereum 2.0 and Cardano. In a staking system, participants, known as validators, lock up a certain amount of cryptocurrency as collateral to validate transactions and secure the network. In return, validators are rewarded with additional coins for their contributions. Staking is seen as a more energy-efficient and environmentally friendly alternative to traditional proof-of-work mining.

Decentralized Finance (DeFi): Decentralized finance, or DeFi, is a rapidly growing sector within the cryptocurrency industry that aims to recreate traditional financial services, such as lending, borrowing, and trading, on decentralized blockchain networks.

Lending and Borrowing: DeFi platforms allow users to lend out their cryptocurrency assets and earn interest on their holdings, or borrow assets by providing collateral. This enables individuals to access financial services without relying on traditional banks or financial institutions.

Decentralized Exchanges (DEXs): DEXs are platforms that facilitate peer-to-peer trading of cryptocurrencies without the need for intermediaries or centralized authorities. By using smart contracts and automated market-making algorithms, DEXs enable users to trade cryptocurrencies directly with one another in a trustless and permissionless manner.

Yield Farming and Liquidity Mining: Yield farming and liquidity mining are strategies used by DeFi participants to earn additional rewards by providing liquidity to decentralized exchanges and lending protocols. By staking their assets in liquidity pools, users can earn fees and rewards in the form of additional tokens.

Non-Fungible Tokens (NFTs):

Non-fungible tokens, or NFTs, are unique digital assets that represent ownership or proof of authenticity of a particular item or piece of content, such as artwork, music, or collectibles. Unlike cryptocurrencies like Bitcoin or Ethereum, which are fungible and can be exchanged on a one-to-one basis, NFTs are indivisible and cannot be replicated or divided.

Digital Art and Collectibles: NFTs have gained popularity in the art world as a way for artists to tokenize and sell their digital artwork as unique collectible items. Platforms like OpenSea and Rarible enable artists to mint and sell NFTs, while collectors can purchase and trade these digital assets on secondary markets.

Gaming and Virtual Worlds: NFTs are also being used in the gaming industry to tokenize in-game assets, such as characters, skins, and virtual real estate. Players can buy, sell, and trade these NFTs on blockchain-based gaming platforms, creating new opportunities for ownership and monetization in virtual worlds.

Case Study: Decentralized Autonomous Organizations (DAOs)

Decentralized Autonomous Organizations (DAOs) are a revolutionary concept in the cryptocurrency space, enabling decentralized governance, decision-making, and management of digital assets through smart contracts and blockchain technology. Let's explore the story of "The DAO," one of the earliest and most infamous DAOs in the cryptocurrency world.

In 2016, "The DAO" was launched on the Ethereum blockchain as a crowdfunding project aimed at creating a decentralized venture capital fund.

The DAO raised over $150 million in Ether (ETH), making it one of the largest crowdfunding campaigns in history at the time.

"The DAO" operated as a decentralized investment fund, allowing token holders to vote on investment proposals and allocate funds to projects within the Ethereum ecosystem. However, the project was plagued by security vulnerabilities and a critical flaw in its smart contract code.

In June 2016, an attacker exploited a loophole in "The DAO" smart contract, siphoning off over $50 million worth of Ether. The incident sparked a contentious debate within the Ethereum community about the principles of decentralization, immutability, and governance.

To mitigate the damage caused by the attack, Ethereum developers proposed a controversial solution known as a "hard fork," which involved rolling back the blockchain to a previous state before the attack occurred. The hard fork resulted in the creation of two separate Ethereum blockchains: Ethereum (ETH) and Ethereum Classic (ETC).

The DAO incident highlighted the potential risks and challenges associated with decentralized autonomous organizations, including security vulnerabilities, code exploits, and governance disputes. Despite the controversy, the concept of DAOs continues to evolve, with new projects exploring innovative models for decentralized governance and decision-making.

By studying the rise and fall of "The DAO," entrepreneurs, developers, and investors can gain valuable insights into the opportunities and pitfalls of decentralized autonomous organizations. DAOs represent a powerful tool for democratizing finance and governance, but they also pose unique challenges that must be addressed to ensure their success and sustainability.

Conclusion:

As the world of cryptocurrencies continues to evolve and mature, advanced topics like mining, staking, DeFi, and NFTs are shaping the future of digital finance and revolutionizing how we interact with money, assets, and digital content. Whether you're interested in participating in consensus mechanisms, exploring new financial opportunities, or collecting unique digital assets, understanding these advanced topics is essential for staying informed and harnessing the full potential of cryptocurrencies in the digital age. So keep exploring, stay curious, and embrace the exciting world of advanced topics in the world of cryptocurrencies.

Chapter 9: Risks and Security Measures

Welcome to the world of risks and security measures in the realm of cryptocurrencies – where innovation meets vulnerability, and protecting your digital assets is paramount. In this chapter, we'll explore the various risks associated with cryptocurrencies and discuss practical security measures you can take to safeguard your investments and protect yourself from threats. Whether you're a seasoned crypto enthusiast or someone who's just getting started, understanding these risks and implementing security best practices is essential for navigating the dynamic and sometimes treacherous landscape of the crypto market.

Risks Associated with Cryptocurrencies:

a. **Volatility:** Cryptocurrencies are notorious for their extreme price volatility, with prices often fluctuating by double-digit percentages in a single day. While volatility can present opportunities for profit, it also exposes investors to the risk of significant losses if not managed properly.

b. **Hacking and Security Breaches:** Cryptocurrency exchanges and wallets are frequent targets for hackers and cybercriminals seeking to steal digital assets. From phishing scams and malware attacks to exchange hacks and data breaches, the crypto industry is rife with security vulnerabilities that can result in the loss of funds.

c. **Regulatory Uncertainty:** The regulatory landscape for cryptocurrencies is constantly evolving, with governments around the world grappling to define their legal status and establish clear regulatory frameworks. Regulatory uncertainty can lead to market volatility and create legal and compliance risks for individuals and businesses operating in the crypto space.

d. **Fraud and Scams:** The anonymous and decentralized nature of cryptocurrencies makes them a ripe target for fraudsters and scammers looking to exploit unsuspecting investors. Ponzi schemes, ICO scams, and fake exchange platforms are just a few examples of the types of fraudulent activities that plague the crypto industry.

Security Measures to Protect Your Investments:

a. Use Secure Wallets: Choose reputable cryptocurrency wallets that offer robust security features, such as multi-factor authentication, encryption, and hardware wallet support. Avoid using online wallets or exchanges as your primary storage solution, as they are more susceptible to hacking and security breaches.

b. Enable Two-Factor Authentication (2FA): Enable 2FA on your wallet and exchange accounts to add an extra layer of security to your login process. This helps prevent unauthorized access to your accounts even if your password is compromised.

c. Keep Your Private Keys Secure: Your private keys are the keys to your crypto kingdom – keep them safe and secure at all times. Store your private keys offline in a secure location, such as a hardware wallet or a paper wallet, and never share them with anyone else.

d. Stay Informed: Stay abreast of the latest security threats and trends in the crypto industry by following reputable news sources, forums, and social media channels. Educate yourself about common security risks and learn how to recognize and avoid potential scams and phishing attacks.

e. Diversify Your Investments: Diversification is key to managing risk in the world of cryptocurrencies. Avoid putting all your eggs in one basket by diversifying your investment portfolio across different cryptocurrencies, industries, and asset classes.

e. ***Practice Good Cyber Hygiene:*** Practice good cyber hygiene by keeping your software and devices up to date with the latest security patches and updates. Use strong, unique passwords for your accounts and consider using a password manager to generate and store your passwords securely.

Case Study: The Mt. Gox Hack

In 2014, Mt. Gox, once the largest Bitcoin exchange in the world, filed for bankruptcy after losing over 850,000 bitcoins, worth approximately $473 million at the time, in a devastating hack. The Mt. Gox hack remains one of the most infamous incidents in the history of cryptocurrencies, underscoring the importance of security measures and risk management in the industry.

Mt. Gox, based in Tokyo, Japan, was founded in 2010 by Jed McCaleb and later acquired by Mark Karpeles. At its peak, Mt. Gox accounted for over 70% of all Bitcoin transactions worldwide, making it a dominant player in the cryptocurrency market.

However, Mt. Gox's success was short-lived, as the exchange faced numerous security breaches and operational challenges over the years. In 2011, Mt. Gox suffered its first major security breach, resulting in the theft of thousands of bitcoins from its hot wallet.

Despite efforts to improve security and restore customer trust, Mt. Gox continued to experience technical issues and liquidity problems. In February 2014, the exchange abruptly halted all withdrawals, citing a critical flaw in its software.

An investigation later revealed that Mt. Gox had been hacked over a period of several years, with hackers exploiting vulnerabilities in the exchange's infrastructure and internal controls. The theft of hundreds of thousands of bitcoins ultimately led to Mt. Gox's collapse and bankruptcy, leaving thousands of customers without access to their funds and sparking a legal and regulatory firestorm in the cryptocurrency industry.

The Mt. Gox hack served as a wake-up call for the cryptocurrency community, highlighting the inherent risks and vulnerabilities associated with centralized exchanges and custodial services. It underscored the need for robust security measures, transparency, and accountability to protect users' funds and maintain the integrity of the ecosystem.

In the aftermath of the Mt. Gox debacle, regulators around the world intensified their scrutiny of cryptocurrency exchanges, imposing stricter compliance requirements and security standards to safeguard investors and prevent similar incidents from occurring in the future. Exchanges also took proactive measures to enhance their security protocols, such as implementing multi-signature wallets, cold storage solutions, and regular security audits.

The Mt. Gox hack remains a cautionary tale for investors and industry stakeholders, emphasizing the importance of conducting due diligence, practicing proper risk management, and exercising vigilance when dealing with cryptocurrency exchanges and third-party custodians. By learning from past mistakes and implementing robust security measures, the cryptocurrency industry can build trust, foster adoption, and pave the way for a more secure and resilient financial ecosystem.

Conclusion:

As the popularity and adoption of cryptocurrencies continue to grow, so too do the risks associated with investing and transacting in digital assets. By understanding the various risks and vulnerabilities in the crypto landscape and implementing robust security measures to protect yourself and your investments, you can navigate the challenges of the crypto market with confidence and resilience. Remember to stay informed, stay vigilant, and stay proactive in safeguarding your digital assets against threats and vulnerabilities. With the right knowledge and precautions, you can enjoy the benefits of cryptocurrencies while minimizing the risks and protecting your financial future in the digital age.

MICHAEL PAGE

Chapter 10: The Future of Cryptocurrencies

Welcome to the final chapter in our journey through the world of cryptocurrencies – where innovation meets possibility, and the future is ripe with potential. In this chapter, we'll explore the exciting prospects and emerging trends that are shaping the future of cryptocurrencies and blockchain technology. Whether you're a seasoned crypto enthusiast or someone who's just getting started, understanding the future of cryptocurrencies is essential for staying ahead of the curve and embracing the opportunities that lie ahead.

Mainstream Adoption:

One of the most promising trends for the future of cryptocurrencies is mainstream adoption. As cryptocurrencies become more widely accepted and integrated into traditional financial systems, they have the potential to revolutionize how we transact, invest, and interact with money. From retail payments and remittances to asset tokenization and decentralized finance (DeFi), cryptocurrencies offer a fast, secure, and borderless alternative to traditional financial services.

Major companies like PayPal, Square, and Visa have already begun to embrace cryptocurrencies, allowing users to buy, sell, and hold digital assets within their platforms. In addition, central banks around the world are exploring the possibility of issuing their own digital currencies, known as central bank digital currencies (CBDCs), as a way to modernize their payment systems and maintain control over monetary policy.

Decentralized Finance (DeFi):

Decentralized finance, or DeFi, is another exciting trend that is shaping the future of cryptocurrencies. DeFi refers to a broad category of financial services and applications built on blockchain networks, such as lending, borrowing, trading, and asset management, that operate without intermediaries or centralized authorities.

Platforms like Compound, Aave, and Uniswap have emerged as leading players in the DeFi space, offering innovative products and services that allow users to earn interest on their crypto assets, borrow against their holdings, and trade digital assets directly with one another. With the rise of DeFi, individuals around the world have access to financial services that were previously unavailable or inaccessible, democratizing access to wealth creation and financial empowerment.

Scalability and Interoperability:

Scalability and interoperability are two key challenges facing blockchain technology as it seeks to achieve mainstream adoption. As the number of transactions and users on blockchain networks continues to grow, scalability becomes increasingly important to ensure that networks can handle the load and process transactions quickly and efficiently.

Several solutions are being developed to address the scalability issue, including layer 2 scaling solutions like the Lightning Network for Bitcoin and the Ethereum 2.0 upgrade, which aims to transition Ethereum from a proof-of-work to a proof-of-stake consensus mechanism. Additionally, interoperability protocols like Polkadot and Cosmos are working to bridge the gap between different blockchain networks, enabling seamless communication and asset transfer between disparate platforms.

Regulation and Compliance:

Regulation and compliance are likely to play a significant role in shaping the future of cryptocurrencies. As governments around the world grapple with the challenges and opportunities presented by cryptocurrencies, we can expect to see increased regulatory scrutiny and oversight of the industry.

While regulation can provide clarity and legitimacy to the crypto market, it also has the potential to stifle innovation and hinder adoption if not implemented thoughtfully. Finding the right balance between regulatory oversight and innovation will be crucial for ensuring the long-term success and sustainability of cryptocurrencies and blockchain technology.

Case Study: Central Bank Digital Currencies (CBDCs)

Central bank digital currencies (CBDCs) have emerged as a key focus area for governments and central banks around the world, representing a potential paradigm shift in the global financial system. Let's explore the case of China's digital yuan, also known as the Digital Currency Electronic Payment (DCEP) project.

In 2014, the People's Bank of China (PBOC) initiated research and development efforts to explore the feasibility of launching a digital currency. The goal was to modernize the country's payment infrastructure, enhance financial inclusion, and bolster the efficiency and security of the financial system.

After years of research and pilot programs, China officially launched the digital yuan pilot in several cities in 2020, marking a significant milestone in the development of CBDCs. The digital yuan operates on a centralized blockchain network controlled by the PBOC, allowing for real-time transactions and settlement between financial institutions and users.

The digital yuan is designed to coexist with existing forms of money and payment systems, offering users a secure, convenient, and efficient means of conducting transactions both online and offline. It also provides the Chinese government with greater visibility and control over the flow of money, enabling more effective monetary policy and financial surveillance.

The rollout of the digital yuan has sparked interest and debate among policymakers, central bankers, and industry stakeholders worldwide, prompting other countries to accelerate their efforts to develop and deploy CBDCs. While CBDCs offer potential benefits such as financial inclusion and efficiency gains, they also raise concerns about privacy, surveillance, and the concentration of power in the hands of central authorities.

The case of China's digital yuan illustrates the evolving landscape of central bank digital currencies and their potential impact on the future of money and finance. As CBDCs continue to gain traction, it is crucial for governments, central banks, and regulators to strike a balance between innovation and regulation to ensure the stability, security, and inclusivity of the global financial system.

By studying the developments and implications of CBDCs, stakeholders can gain valuable insights into the future of cryptocurrencies, digital payments, and the broader financial ecosystem. The adoption of CBDCs represents a significant milestone in the ongoing digital transformation of the global economy, with far-reaching implications for monetary policy, financial stability, and economic sovereignty.

Conclusion:

The future of cryptocurrencies is bright and full of promise, with the potential to revolutionize how we transact, invest, and interact with money in the digital age. From mainstream adoption and decentralized finance to scalability and interoperability, the opportunities for growth and innovation in the crypto space are endless.

MICHAEL PAGE

As we look ahead to the future of cryptocurrencies, it's important to stay informed, stay curious, and stay engaged with the latest developments and trends in the industry. Whether you're a developer building the next generation of decentralized applications, an investor looking to capitalize on emerging opportunities, or simply someone curious about the potential of blockchain technology, the future of cryptocurrencies is yours to shape and explore. So embrace the possibilities, stay open to new ideas, and remember that the best is yet to come in the world of cryptocurrencies.

Interview Questions with Responses from Michael Page

Question: What do you believe are the most significant challenges facing the cryptocurrency industry today, and how can they be addressed?

Michael Page: One of the biggest challenges facing the cryptocurrency industry is regulatory uncertainty. Governments around the world are still grappling with how to classify and regulate cryptocurrencies, which creates uncertainty for businesses and investors. To address this challenge, industry stakeholders need to work closely with regulators to develop clear and balanced regulations that promote innovation while protecting consumers and investors.

Question: What are your thoughts on the recent surge in interest and investment in decentralized finance (DeFi) platforms, and do you see this trend continuing in the future?

Michael Page: The growth of decentralized finance has been remarkable, with billions of dollars locked in DeFi platforms and protocols. This trend is driven by the desire for greater financial inclusion, transparency, and control over one's assets. I believe that DeFi has the potential to revolutionize traditional finance by providing open, permissionless access to financial services. However, it's essential to address challenges such as scalability, security, and regulatory compliance to ensure the long-term sustainability of the DeFi ecosystem.

Question: With the rise of non-fungible tokens (NFTs) and digital art marketplaces, what opportunities do you see for artists, collectors, and investors in the cryptocurrency space?

Michael Page: The emergence of NFTs has opened up new opportunities for artists to monetize their work and reach a global audience without relying on traditional intermediaries. NFTs enable artists to tokenize their creations, establish ownership rights, and monetize digital assets in ways that were previously impossible. For collectors and investors, NFTs offer a unique opportunity to own and trade digital assets with provable scarcity and authenticity. As the NFT ecosystem continues to evolve, we can expect to see even more innovative use cases and applications emerge.

Question: What role do you believe central bank digital currencies (CBDCs) will play in shaping the future of money and finance, and how should businesses and individuals prepare for this paradigm shift?

Michael Page: Central bank digital currencies represent a significant evolution in the global monetary system, with the potential to streamline payments, enhance financial inclusion, and facilitate cross-border transactions. Businesses and individuals should prepare for the advent of CBDCs by familiarizing themselves with digital currencies, understanding the implications for their business models and financial transactions, and staying informed about regulatory developments. While CBDCs offer exciting opportunities, they also raise important questions about privacy, security, and financial sovereignty that need to be addressed.

Question: What do you see as the most promising use cases for blockchain technology beyond cryptocurrencies, and how do you envision blockchain shaping industries such as supply chain management, healthcare, and real estate?

Michael Page: Blockchain technology has the potential to revolutionize a wide range of industries beyond cryptocurrencies. In supply chain management, blockchain can provide transparency, traceability, and immutability of transactions, reducing fraud, counterfeiting, and inefficiencies in global supply chains. In healthcare, blockchain can improve data security, interoperability, and patient privacy, enabling secure sharing and access to medical records and healthcare data. In real estate, blockchain can streamline property transactions, reduce friction, and automate processes such as title transfers and land registries. Overall, blockchain holds tremendous promise for transforming industries and creating new opportunities for innovation and efficiency.

Practical Tips and Strategies for Beginners

Here are some practical tips and strategies for beginners to navigate the cryptocurrency market safely and effectively:

Educate Yourself:

Before diving into the cryptocurrency market, take the time to educate yourself about blockchain technology, cryptocurrencies, and the underlying principles of digital finance. There are many resources available online, including articles, tutorials, and courses, that can help you build a solid foundation of knowledge.

Start Small:

Begin by investing only **what you can afford to lose**. Cryptocurrency markets can be highly volatile, and prices can fluctuate dramatically in a short period. Start with a small investment and gradually increase your exposure as you gain confidence and experience in the market.

Diversify Your Portfolio:

Diversification is key to managing risk in the cryptocurrency market. Instead of putting all your eggs in one basket, consider diversifying your investment across different cryptocurrencies, asset classes, and investment strategies. This can help mitigate the impact of market volatility and reduce the risk of significant losses.

Practice Good Security Habits:

Protect your cryptocurrency holdings by practicing good security habits. Use hardware wallets or secure software wallets to store your digital assets, and enable two-factor authentication (2FA) for added security. Be cautious of phishing scams, malware, and fraudulent schemes designed to steal your private keys or passwords.

Stay Updated with Market Trends:

Keep yourself informed about market trends, news, and developments in the cryptocurrency industry. Follow reputable sources such as cryptocurrency news websites, forums, and social media channels to stay updated on the latest market movements, regulatory changes, and technological advancements.

Set Realistic Goals:

Define your investment goals and develop a clear investment strategy based on your risk tolerance, time horizon, and financial objectives. Set realistic expectations and avoid chasing quick profits or falling for hype-driven investment opportunities.

Monitor Your Investments:

Regularly monitor your cryptocurrency investments and assess their performance against your investment goals. Stay disciplined and avoid making impulsive decisions based on short-term market fluctuations. Consider using portfolio tracking tools or spreadsheets to keep track of your investments and performance over time.

Stay Patient and Persistent:

Investing in cryptocurrencies requires patience and persistence. The market can be unpredictable, and prices may experience significant fluctuations in the short term. Stay focused on your long-term investment goals and resist the urge to panic sell or make emotional decisions based on fear or greed.

Seek Professional Advice if Needed:

If you're unsure about where to start or how to navigate the cryptocurrency market, consider seeking advice from a financial advisor or cryptocurrency expert. They can provide personalized guidance, help you assess your risk tolerance, and develop an investment strategy tailored to your individual needs and circumstances.

Stay Humble and Keep Learning:

Finally, remember that investing in cryptocurrencies is a journey, not a destination. Stay humble, keep learning, and adapt to changes in the market and technology. By continuously educating yourself and staying informed, you can navigate the cryptocurrency market safely and effectively over the long term.

Conclusion

Congratulations! You've reached the end of our journey through the fascinating world of cryptocurrencies. Whether you're a seasoned crypto enthusiast or someone who's just beginning to dip their toes into the digital waters, I hope this exploration has provided you with valuable insights and inspiration for navigating the exciting and ever-evolving landscape of cryptocurrencies.

As we wrap up our discussion, let's take a moment to reflect on the key takeaways and lessons learned from our exploration:

Empowerment Through Knowledge: Cryptocurrencies offer a unique opportunity for individuals to take control of their financial future and participate in the global economy on their own terms. By understanding the fundamentals of cryptocurrencies, blockchain technology, and the various use cases and applications, you can empower yourself to make informed decisions and leverage the transformative potential of digital money.

Diversity and Innovation: The world of cryptocurrencies is vast and diverse, with thousands of different projects, platforms, and technologies pushing the boundaries of innovation and creativity. From Bitcoin and Ethereum to decentralized finance (DeFi) and non-fungible tokens (NFTs), there's something for everyone in the crypto space, regardless of your interests or background.

Risk and Responsibility: While cryptocurrencies offer exciting opportunities for wealth creation and financial empowerment, they also come with risks and challenges that should not be overlooked. From price volatility and security vulnerabilities to regulatory uncertainty and market manipulation, navigating the crypto landscape requires diligence, caution, and a willingness to learn from both successes and setbacks.

Community and Collaboration: At its core, the success of cryptocurrencies depends on the strength of the community and the spirit of collaboration that drives innovation and progress in the industry. Whether you're a developer building the next generation of decentralized applications, an investor supporting promising projects, or simply someone curious about the potential of blockchain technology, your contributions and engagement are vital to shaping the future of cryptocurrencies.

The Future is Bright: Despite the challenges and uncertainties that lie ahead, the future of cryptocurrencies is bright and full of promise. With mainstream adoption on the rise, decentralized finance revolutionizing traditional financial services, and emerging technologies like scalability solutions and interoperability protocols pushing the boundaries of what's possible, the opportunities for growth and innovation in the crypto space are endless.

As you continue your journey in the world of cryptocurrencies, I encourage you to stay curious, stay informed, and stay engaged with the latest developments and trends in the industry. Whether you're exploring new investment opportunities, building innovative applications, or simply seeking to understand the transformative potential of blockchain technology, the world of cryptocurrencies is yours to explore and shape.

Remember, the journey doesn't end

here – it's just the beginning of an exciting and transformative adventure in the digital age. So embrace the possibilities, seize the opportunities, and continue to push the boundaries of what's possible in the world of cryptocurrencies. The future is yours to create – so go forth and make it extraordinary!

Happy hodling, and may the blockchain be with you.

MICHAEL PAGE

Glossary

This glossary provides a basic understanding of common terms used in the cryptocurrency industry and can serve as a reference for readers as they explore the world of digital finance.

Airdrop: A marketing strategy used by cryptocurrency projects to distribute free tokens or coins to existing holders of a specific cryptocurrency. Airdrops are often used to increase awareness, incentivize participation, and reward loyal supporters of the project.

Altcoin: Any cryptocurrency other than Bitcoin. Altcoins may have unique features, use cases, or consensus mechanisms different from Bitcoin.

Atomic Swap: A peer-to-peer exchange of cryptocurrencies between two parties without the need for intermediaries or centralized exchanges.

Atomic swaps use smart contracts to ensure that either both parties receive the agreed-upon assets or the transaction is canceled and funds are returned to the original owners.

Blockchain: A distributed ledger technology that records transactions across multiple computers in a decentralized network, ensuring transparency, immutability, and security.

Consensus: The process by which participants in a blockchain network agree on the validity of transactions and the state of the blockchain. Consensus mechanisms, such as proof of work (PoW) and proof of stake (PoS), ensure that all nodes in the network reach a common understanding of the blockchain's state.

Cryptocurrency: A digital or virtual currency that uses cryptography for security and operates on decentralized networks based on blockchain technology.

DApp (Decentralized Application): An application that runs on a decentralized blockchain network and is powered by smart contracts. DApps are designed to be open-source, transparent, and resistant to censorship and tampering.

Decentralized Autonomous Organization (DAO): An organization governed by smart contracts and run on a decentralized blockchain network. DAOs operate autonomously and transparently, with decisions made by consensus among token holders based on predefined rules and protocols.

Decentralized Finance (DeFi): A rapidly growing sector within the cryptocurrency industry that aims to recreate traditional financial services, such as lending, borrowing, and trading, on decentralized blockchain networks.

Exchange: A platform where users can buy, sell, and trade cryptocurrencies for other digital or fiat currencies. Examples include Coinbase, Binance, and Kraken.

FOMO (Fear of Missing Out): A psychological phenomenon where individuals experience anxiety or fear of missing out on potential opportunities or gains in the cryptocurrency market. FOMO can influence investors' decisions to buy or sell assets based on emotional impulses rather than rational analysis.

Fork: A split in the blockchain, resulting in two separate chains with a shared history. Forks can be classified as hard forks (irreversible split) or soft forks (backward-compatible split).

Fork Delta: A decentralized cryptocurrency exchange (DEX) built on the Ethereum blockchain that allows users to trade ERC-20 tokens directly from their Ethereum wallets. Fork Delta operates without intermediaries or centralized control, providing users with greater privacy and security.

Forking: The process of creating a new blockchain protocol by copying an existing blockchain and making changes to its codebase. Forks can occur for various reasons, such as protocol upgrades, disagreements among developers, or to create a new cryptocurrency.

Gas: A unit of measurement for the computational work required to execute operations or transactions on a blockchain network. Users must pay gas fees to miners or validators to process transactions and smart contracts on the network.

Hard Wallet: Another term for a hardware wallet, which is a physical device used to securely store cryptocurrencies offline. Hard wallets are considered one of the most secure methods for storing digital assets.

Hash Function: A mathematical algorithm that converts input data into a fixed-size string of characters, typically used to secure transactions and verify the integrity of data on the blockchain.

HODL: A slang term derived from a misspelling of "hold," which refers to the strategy of holding onto cryptocurrencies for the long term without selling, regardless of short-term price fluctuations. HODLers believe in the long-term potential and value of their investments.

ICO (Initial Coin Offering): A fundraising method used by cryptocurrency startups to raise capital by issuing new tokens or coins to investors in exchange for funding. Investors typically purchase these tokens with existing cryptocurrencies like Bitcoin or Ethereum.

Immutable: A characteristic of blockchain technology where once a transaction is recorded on the blockchain, it cannot be altered or deleted. Immutability ensures the integrity and security of the blockchain by preventing unauthorized changes to transaction history.

KYC (Know Your Customer): A regulatory process used by financial institutions and cryptocurrency exchanges to verify the identity of their customers and assess their risk profile. KYC procedures typically involve collecting personal information and documentation from customers to comply with anti-money laundering (AML) and counter-terrorism financing (CTF) regulations.

Liquidity: A measure of how easily and quickly an asset, such as a cryptocurrency, can be bought or sold in the market without significantly affecting its price. High liquidity indicates a deep and active market with ample trading volume and low transaction costs.

Mining: The process of validating and adding new transactions to the blockchain by solving complex mathematical puzzles. Miners use powerful computers to compete for the chance to add a new block to the blockchain and receive rewards in the form of newly minted coins.

Multi-Signature (Multisig): A security feature that requires multiple private keys to authorize transactions or access funds in a cryptocurrency wallet. Multisig wallets are considered more secure than single-signature wallets and are often used for shared custody and escrow services.

Node: A computer or device that participates in the operation of a blockchain network by maintaining a copy of the blockchain and validating transactions. Nodes can be full nodes, which store the entire blockchain, or light nodes, which rely on full nodes to verify transactions.

Non-Fungible Token (NFT): A unique digital asset that represents ownership or proof of authenticity of a particular item or piece of content, such as artwork, music, or collectibles, on the blockchain.

Peer-to-Peer (P2P): A decentralized communication model where participants interact directly with each other without the need for intermediaries or central authorities. Cryptocurrencies operate on P2P networks, allowing users to transact directly with one another without the need for banks or financial institutions.

Private Key: A secret cryptographic key that allows users to access and control their cryptocurrencies. It must be kept confidential and securely stored to prevent unauthorized access.

Proof of Stake (PoS): A consensus mechanism used by some blockchain networks, such as Ethereum 2.0, where validators are chosen to create new blocks and secure the network based on the amount of cryptocurrency they hold and are willing to "stake" as collateral.

Proof of Work (PoW): A consensus mechanism used by some blockchain networks, such as Bitcoin, where miners must solve cryptographic puzzles to validate transactions and secure the network.

Public Key: A cryptographic key that serves as an address for receiving cryptocurrencies. It is derived from the private key and can be shared publicly without compromising security.

Pump and Dump: A market manipulation scheme where the price of a cryptocurrency is artificially inflated (pumped) by coordinated buying, followed by selling (dumping) to profit from the price increase. Pump and dump schemes often target low-volume and low-market-cap cryptocurrencies.

Smart Contract: Self-executing contracts with the terms of the agreement directly written into code. Smart contracts automatically execute and enforce the terms of the agreement when predefined conditions are met.

Smart Wallet: A type of cryptocurrency wallet that incorporates advanced features and functionality, such as support for smart contracts, decentralized applications (DApps), and automated transactions. Smart wallets aim to enhance the user experience and enable advanced use cases beyond basic storage and transfer of funds.

Soft Wallet: Another term for a software wallet, which is a digital wallet application or program that allows users to store, send, and receive cryptocurrencies on their computer or mobile device.

Stablecoin: A type of cryptocurrency designed to maintain a stable value by pegging its value to a fiat currency, commodity, or algorithmic mechanism. Stablecoins are often used for trading, hedging against volatility, and as a medium of exchange.

Token: A digital asset issued on a blockchain network that represents a unit of value or ownership. Tokens can serve various purposes, such as utility tokens for accessing a platform or security tokens representing ownership in an asset.

Tokenomics: The economic model and principles governing the issuance, distribution, and management of tokens within a cryptocurrency ecosystem. Tokenomics encompasses factors such as token supply, distribution mechanisms, utility, and value proposition.

Wallet: A software program or hardware device that allows users to store, send, and receive cryptocurrencies. Wallets can be online (hot wallets), offline (cold wallets), or paper wallets.

Wallet Address: A string of alphanumeric characters used to send or receive cryptocurrencies. It serves as a destination for sending funds and is derived from the public key.

Wallet Seed Phrase: A series of randomly generated words used to back up and restore a cryptocurrency wallet. The seed phrase allows users to recover their wallet and access their funds in case the original wallet is lost or damaged.

Whale: A term used to describe individuals or entities that hold large amounts of cryptocurrencies. Whales have the potential to influence market prices through their buying or selling activities.

White Hat Hacker: A cybersecurity expert or ethical hacker who uses their skills and knowledge to identify and fix security vulnerabilities in computer systems and networks. White hat hackers play a crucial role in improving the security of blockchain networks and protecting against malicious attacks.

Whitepaper: A formal document issued by a cryptocurrency project or company that outlines its mission, technology, tokenomics, and plans for development and deployment. Whitepapers are commonly used to attract investors and stakeholders to the project.

Zero-Knowledge Proof (ZKP): A cryptographic technique that allows one party to prove the validity of a statement or transaction to another party without revealing any sensitive information. ZKPs are used to enhance privacy and confidentiality in blockchain transactions while maintaining transparency and integrity.

About the Author

Michael Page is a passionate advocate for blockchain technology and cryptocurrencies. With a background in finance and technology, Michael has been actively involved in the cryptocurrency space for several years. He is committed to educating and empowering individuals to navigate the complexities of the digital finance landscape safely and effectively.

Through his writing and speaking engagements, Michael aims to demystify cryptocurrencies and help beginners embark on their journey to financial freedom. When he's not immersed in the world of blockchain, Michael enjoys hiking, photography, and spending time with his family.

Printed in Great Britain
by Amazon

c2721cc4-0e8e-424e-aa53-df8a4852e708R01